Secret Gardens of Paris *is dedicated to my late*
mother Elpida, who possessed a natural green thumb, able to nurture
almost anything into bloom — from flourishing orchards to an olive tree
that miraculously sprouted from her compost!

Elli Ioannou, Paris

ELLI IOANNOU

SECRET GARDENS OF PARIS

CONTENTS

RIGHT BANK – RIVE DROITE
116

SECRET

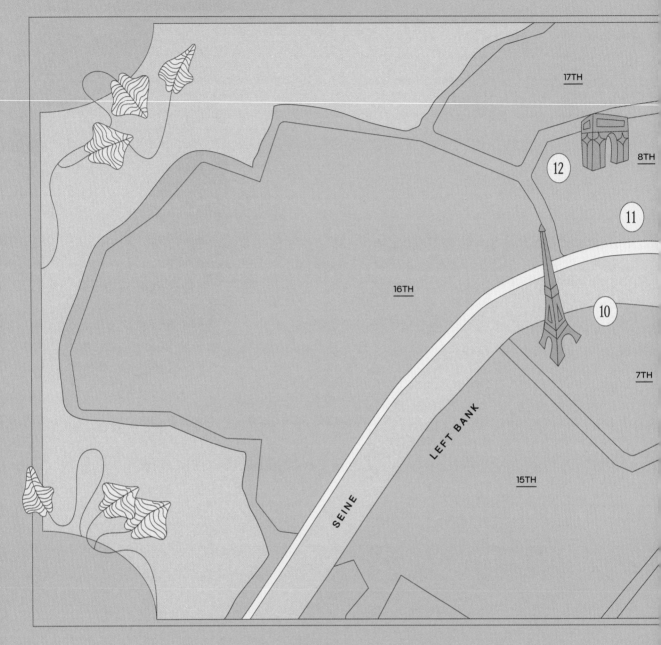

17TH

8TH

12

11

16TH

10

LEFT BANK

7TH

SEINE

15TH

LEFT BANK — RIVE GAUCHE

GARDENS

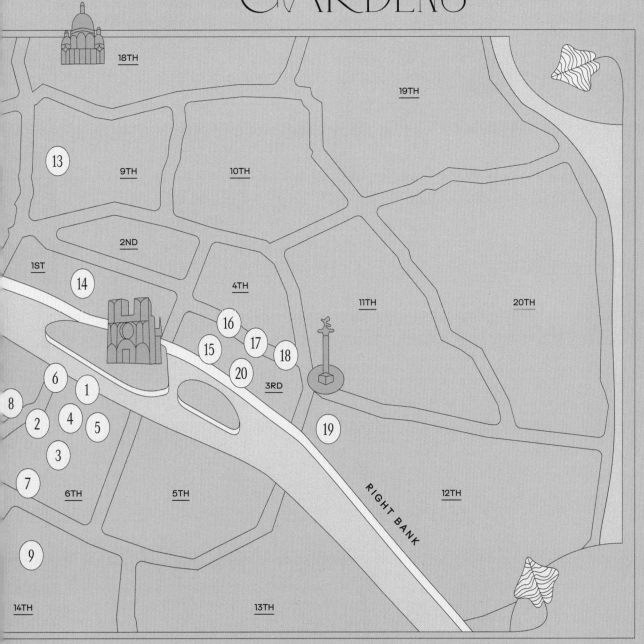

18TH

19TH

13

9TH

10TH

2ND

1ST

14

4TH

11TH

20TH

16

17

15

18

20

3RD

6

1

8

19

2

4

5

3

7

12TH

6TH

5TH

9

14TH

13TH

RIGHT BANK — RIVE DROITE

INTRODUCTION

When I first moved to Paris from Melbourne, Australia, I missed the sense of being close to nature, but in exploring my new home, I soon discovered a genuine Parisian commitment to green space. My appreciation for nature and gardens as a place to retreat and to create a sense of belonging is also influenced by my own mother's love for the garden she created in our home in Australia, so this was very welcome.

From the Bois de Boulogne on the west of the city to the Bois de Vincennes at the east, from the Jardin du Luxembourg to the Tuileries Gardens, large formal parks in Paris exist, but what surprised and delighted me were the myriad secret green spaces dotted throughout the busy streets. I quickly found that I was never far from little squares or secluded gardens, public squares, museum gardens or hotel courtyards. All provided somewhere I could sit for

a moment, to pause and be inspired, read, reflect or meditate. And this is available for you, too.

These 'secret gardens' and green spaces are more than just a part of urban design; they present a truly Parisian cultural experience, an invitation to step into another timeline of history. Each one included in this book offers a relaxed way to learn about the rich history of Paris, often through art and literature, but also through the people after whom some of these spaces are named. Many include original sculptures by artists, including the delightful surprise of a Picasso in Square Laurent-Prache.

There is well-documented research on the benefits of nature to our mental health. It helps shift perspective, enhances positive thinking, reduces stress and can alleviate anxiety and depression. Whatever your mood, it can always be improved by taking time out among trees and plants.

The City of Paris has a policy of 'greening' its environment, aiming to become a 'garden city'. Over 100,000 trees have been planted since 2020, and many asphalt surfaces have been replaced with innovative new materials that can help mitigate climate change. The emphasis is on preserving biodiversity, reducing air pollution, protecting the city from heatwaves and providing access to green space within 15 minutes' walk from home for everyone. The Coulée Verte René-Dumont is one such example: an urban railway converted to an extensive corridor of green.

Secret gardens could be found everywhere when you know to look out for them – on street corners, like Jardin Auguste Scheurer-Kestner, or tucked into hotel courtyards, like Le Pavillon de la Reine. They can exist as an extensive sequence of modern planting that reflects the indigenous *objets d'art* at Le Musée du Quai Branly – Jacques Chirac, or a cleverly designed 'paper garden' that resonates with the preservation of books and manuscripts at Le Jardin Vivienne, BNF Richelieu.

Museum gardens can have a special resonance. One of my choices for this book is the Musée Bourdelle, which I first visited in 2017 to see an exhibition on Cristóbal Balenciaga, *Balenciaga: L'oeuvre au noir*. Balenciaga's exquisite haute couture designs were exhibited in the museum's galleries alongside architectural pieces, huge sculptures and other artefacts designed to mirror the sculptural effect of his creations, fostering a contemporary dialogue between the designer and the artist Antoine Bourdelle, two creative masters from two different periods. I then found its beautiful sequence of gardens – a real discovery of green walkways and peaceful seating, dotted with further statues – to admire.

Trees feature in every garden space in this book, whether small or large, newly planted or spanning the centuries. It may be a fig tree dating from the 1920s in Square Georges-Cain, a towering weeping beech in Square Roger-Stéphane, the *Paulownia* trees in the garden of the Musée Bourdelle and Place de Furstemberg, the flowering lilacs and graceful silver birches or the pollarded chestnut trees and more exotic acacias – the trees in Paris flourish and show us the changing cycles of the seasons. For me, the prominent trees at the entrance of the Musée de la Vie Romantique are a highlight, while a single tree marks the creation of Paris's smallest public garden, Jardin Alice Saunier Seïté.

As the seasons change, so do the gardens. Glazed by frost, misted by rain or dazzled by sunlight, the fresh green colours of the spring, the abundance of flowers in the summer, or the glowing decline of autumn – the pleasures are year-round. Meet a friend, enjoy a coffee, tisane or aperitif, as many of the gardens have cafés or pop-up restaurants in the summer. You can socialise or people-watch alone, read a book or just be mindful of the beauty, but the gardens of Paris will always be a source of inspiration and delight.

Elli Ioannou

LEFT BANK
RIVE GAUCHE

The beautiful river Seine runs through the centre of the city and neatly divides Paris into the Left and Right Banks, and Parisians will often identify themselves by the side of the river on which they live. It is a label that reflects not just *where* they live, but also their attitude to life and their lifestyle. To the outsider, it may seem inconsequential, but there are often playful yet sincere debates about which side of the city is more stylish, sophisticated or simply better – Rive Gauche or Rive Droite.

Rive Gauche has long been associated with the intellectual and free-thinking side of Paris. This reputation is not just because of the famous Sorbonne Université, but also because in the 1920s, writers and artists like Ernest Hemingway, Henry Miller, James Joyce and Gertrude Stein embraced the lively and creative atmosphere of the Left Bank, celebrating its avant-garde lifestyle.

Jean-Paul Sartre and Simone de Beauvoir often met at Café de Flore or Les Deux Magots in Place Saint-Germain-des-Prés, where they discussed philosophy, smoked and drank. In 1966, Yves Saint Laurent was the first couturier to launch a ready-to-wear boutique under his name on the Rue de Tournon, naming it 'Rive Gauche' to reflect the Left Bank's free-spirited yet intellectual vibe.

Some iconic films were also filmed in the Left Bank, including Jean-Luc Godard's 1960 film *Breathless*, using locations along the riverfront directly opposite the Notre-Dame de Paris, the awe-inspiring cathedral so easily recognised by audiences. And in Martin Scorsese's 1993 film *The Age of Innocence*, Place de Furstemberg appears in the last scene of the film.

Saint-Germain-des-Prés, considered to be the heart of the Rive Gauche, exudes elegance. The main Boulevard Saint-Germain is lined with classic café terraces, luxury boutiques, ivy-covered railings and gourmet restaurants. And round the École des Beaux-Arts, you'll find antique shops, art galleries and small hidden museums tucked into quiet squares.

More than anything, the Left Bank keeps its intellectual and artistic spirit alive with its many bookstores, cinemas and lecture halls. The Rive Gauche maintains a mix of history and modern life, its cachet continuing to attract people to the south side of the Seine.

SQUARE GABRIEL-PIERNÉ

ADDRESS 5 Rue de Seine, 75006

HOURS 8/9 a.m. to 5.00 p.m.

METRO Saint-Germain-de-Prés

A short walk from the famous lovers' bridge, the Pont des Arts, and tucked behind the Institut de France, with its domed roof visible above the treeline, is this small treasure of a square.

Originally known as Square de la Rue Mazarine, it was renamed in 1969 in honour of the renowned French composer, conductor and pianist Gabriel Pierné (1863–1937), who had lived nearby.

There are several distinctive features in the square. Among the stone benches are two limestone ones fashioned into open books, a design that acknowledges the literary and artistic heritage of the area, in particular the Bibliothèque Mazarine – the library of the Institut de France – and the art galleries and bookstores of Saint-Germain-de-Prés.

The Fontaine de Fragonard, dating back to 1830, was recognized as a 'monument historique' in 1952. It features a column with a symbolic sculpture showing two faces that represent trade and abundance. Sculpted by Alexandre-Évariste Fragonard (1780–1850, the son of the painter Jean-Honoré Fragonard), it was originally commissioned for the Marché des Carmes in the 5th arrondissement, but was relocated here after the market's demolition in 1930.

Another statue, a bronze of a young naked girl, was erected in 1968, but initially proved controversial. It depicts the daughter of sculptor Marcello Tommasi (1928–2008), and is known as 'Carolina'.

The cherry trees here create an abundance of blossom in the spring when the square celebrates its own hanami, the Japanese tradition of simply 'looking at flowers'. Beneath the magnolia trees lining the square's only wall lies an eco garden, thoughtfully designed to support birds and insects. The garden includes a composting system maintained by the council. Enjoyed by local residents as much as visiting tourists, this square has a real Parisian ambience and is one of many that contribute to the current mayoral policy to create a greener city.

LEFT Fontaine de Fragonard, 1830.

ABOVE View of the dome of Institut de France from within the square.

RIGHT Book-shaped stone bench with Fontaine de Fragonard
in the background.

2

SQUARE LAURENT-PRACHE

ADDRESS 1 Place Saint-Germain-de-Prés, 75006

HOURS 9.30 a.m. to 5.00 p.m.

METRO Saint-Germain-des-Prés

Only a stone's throw from the bustling Boulevard de Saint-Germain, this square nestles behind the Église de Saint-Germain -de-Prés, which was built on the site of a former Benedictine abbey, the ancient arcades of its Chapelle de la Vierge providing a backdrop to the square.

It's hard to miss the acknowledgement to singer Juliette Gréco (1927–2020) on its railings, and entering through its elegant gatework immediately ahead is an original bronze Picasso, a bust of his former lover Dora Maar. Picasso gifted this to the city of Paris in 1959 in homage to his friend, French poet and playwright Guillaume Apollinaire (1880–1918), who died of Spanish flu at home at 202 Boulevard de Saint-Germain. The bronze was stolen in 1999 and not recovered until 2001, after being discovered in a ditch and exhibited in the town hall of Osny, whose inhabitants were initially unaware of its origins, some 30 kilometres from Paris.

Laurent Prache (1856–1919), after whom the square is named, was a French politician and deputy mayor of Paris. He is honoured by a commemorative plaque and a marble portrait in relief by François de Hérain (1877–1962), a French doctor, who was also a sculptor and painter.

The square is situated in one of the most prestigious areas of Paris, known for its luxury boutiques and galleries and for the nearby café Les Deux Magots, which first opened its doors in 1884 and was patronised by the likes of Picasso, Hemingway, Simone de Beauvoir, Camus and James Joyce, continuing to enhance the area's literary and artistic milieu.

The square is also home to one of the city's 107 Wallace drinking fountains, an initiative gifted to the city by English philanthropist Sir Richard Wallace (1818–1890) who financed, created and donated an initial 50 fountains, their purpose being to provide access to clean drinking water for everyone.

Garden beds are planted seasonally, ensuring a colourful turnover throughout the year - alongside the red and white horse chestnut trees, there is a Judas tree, yew tree, Mexican orange blossoms and rhododendrons. For local residents, shopworkers and casual visitors alike, it creates something of a sanctuary, sheltered and peaceful.

21

3

SQUARE FÉLIX DESRUELLES

ADDRESS 168 bis Boulevard de Saint-Germain, 75006

HOURS 8/9 a.m. to 5.45 p.m.

METRO Mabillon/Saint-Germain-des-Prés

Located literally on the boulevard, in the grounds of the Église de Saint-Germain-de-Prés, this square is named after the sculptor Félix-Alexandre Desruelles (1865–1943), a member of the prestigious Académie des Beaux-Arts and known for his many First World War memorials. On the west wall of the square is Desruelles' own work, *La Fontaine Pastorale*, depicting a shepherd with two sheep and a young woman. It's carved from Chavigny stone, a French limestone, and its base has three water outlets flowing into a trough.

Perhaps the most famous feature is the art nouveau arch to the east of the garden: 12 metres high and 10 metres wide, it was originally built for the 1900 Paris Exposition. It is now attached to the wall of an adjoining building. The arch was created by architect Charles Risler (1864–1937) and sculptor Jules Coutan (1848–1939), and was designed to showcase all the skill and artistic virtuosity of the ceramic workshops of the Manufacture Nationale de Sèvres. After the exposition closed, it was installed in the square in 1905.

Another statue that also reflects expertise in ceramics is that of Renaissance man Bernard Palissy (1509–1590), the French Huguenot potter and writer. He developed rusticware, now known as Palissy pottery – beautiful earthenware ceramics with coloured lead glazes often depicting animals, plants and allegorical scenes. His work can still be found in numerous museum collections, like that of the Victoria and Albert Museum in London. There's also a slide and climbing bars in the square, for the enjoyment of the children of today.

For such a tiny garden, it packs quite the punch, and benefits from lush greenery in the summer months, providing seating and welcome shade for its visitors.

28

ABOVE 'Sevres' Art Nouveau ceramic portico, 1900.

RIGHT 'Fontaine Pastorale' by Félix Desruelles, 1925.

29

ABOVE Lower detail of 'Sevres' Art Nouveau ceramic portico.

RIGHT Full-scale view of 'Sevres' Art Nouveau ceramic portico.

33

34

36

4

MUSÉE NATIONAL EUGÈNE-DELACROIX

ADDRESS 6 Rue de Furstemberg, 75006

HOURS 9.30 a.m. to 5.30 p.m., closed Tuesdays

METRO Saint-Germain-des-Prés

37

Although access to this garden is so secret that it's via the museum, for which you need to pay, it's well worth it – as is seeing the Romantic artist Eugène Delacroix's studio. It became a national museum in 1971, and since 2004 has been under the auspices of the Musée du Louvre.

Delacroix had moved to this area from the Nouvelle-Athènes district in the 9th arrondissement in 1857, to be closer to the Église Saint-Sulpice, where he had been commissioned to paint three murals in the Chapelle de la Vierge. 'My apartment is decidedly charming ... Woke up the next day to see the most gracious sun on the houses opposite my window. The view of my little garden and the cheerful appearance of my studio always make me happy', he wrote in his journal on 28 December 1857.

We also know from a recovered memorandum that Delacroix 'restored the soil, pruned and trimmed the existing beds and vines, created flower beds lined with thyme and planted a large number of various rose bushes, redcurrants, raspberry bushes and several trees'.

In 2012, Pierre Bonnaure, then the head gardener at the Tuileries, was able to work from details mined from Delacroix's own writings in order to make the restoration as close to the original as possible. Mature trees, hedged flower beds, fruit bushes, seasonal planting and abundant roses helped to create the sense of a lush, country-style garden that was so close to Delacroix's heart. In doing so, Bonnaure's team have managed to recreate the tranquillity that the garden afforded the artist, which it continues to offer its present-day visitors.

Access to the museum is via Place de Furstemberg, considered one of Paris's most charming spots thanks to its mature *Paulownia* trees, which produce fragrant floral blossoms in the spring. At its centre, there's an ornate five-globe lamp post, adding to the romance of this residential square that appears in several movies, including Vincente Minnelli's *Gigi* (1958) and Martin Scorsese's *The Age of Innocence* (1993). Numerous ground-floor shops include a florist, and its abundant stock of flowers and plants are displayed on the pavement, amplifying the garden feel.

38

44

5

JARDIN AUGUSTE SCHEURER -KESTNER

ADDRESS 2 Rue Jacob, 75006

HOURS Not open to the public

METRO Saint Germain des Prés/Mabillon

45

This beautiful spot is more of a green space than a garden, as it is gated and not accessible to anyone. While a monument to the man after whom this garden is named, Auguste Scheurer-Kestner (1833–1899), is in the famed and extensive Jardin du Luxembourg, there is a reason why this tiny green oasis at the junction of Rue Jacob, Rue de Seine and Rue de l'Echaudé is named after him. A renowned industrialist, Republican and senator in the Third French Republic, he defended Captain Alfred Dreyfus (1859–1935), who'd been wrongly accused of treason in a trial that became known as the Dreyfus Affair.

Central to the garden is a spherical brass water fountain, the work of Guy Lartigue (1927–2021), who produced over 80 public works, many of which are fountains. This one is surrounded by a fig, a palm and poplar trees, flowering grasses and bamboo, lending an oriental feel to this small green space. Even if it's not possible to enter or sit in the garden, just chancing upon its tranquil water feature provides a moment to pause and feel calm.

The streets around it include contemporary art galleries and upmarket boutiques, and opposite is 57 Rue de Seine, built in 1740 for Henri Diéval, a master printer, with beautifully ornate and balconied windows and flower boxes on its second floor. In 1885, it was the Hôtel du Maroc, where poet Charles Baudelaire (1821–1867) stayed for several months; and in 1902, a penniless Pablo Picasso (1881–1973) shared an attic room with the sculptor August Agero (1880–1945).

But in the 1970s, the basement was home to the infamous Rock'n' Roll Circus nightclub, frequented by Mick Jagger and other stars, including Jim Morrison, front man for The Doors. According to Bob Seymore, in his 1991 book *The End: The Death of Jim Morrison*, rock journalist Sam Bernett, who was working at the club on the night of Morrison's death, said it was here that he died from a drug overdose on 3 July 1971. For many Morrison fans, this address forms part of their pilgrimage.

In the evenings, the back wall of this lovely green space is transformed into a modern urban-art installation by a colourful light show, in a nod to its artistic contribution to the area.

6

SQUARE ALICE SAUNIER-SEÏTÉ

ADDRESS 10 Rue Visconti, 75006

HOURS 24 hours (except for maintenance)

METRO Saint-Germain-des-Prés

53

The smallest of Paris's squares on this 16th-century street was originally named Square Visconti, but in October 2017, it became Square Alice Saunier-Seïté (1925–2003). She was a geographer, historian, university professor and politician, and also the first female Secretary of State for Universities between 1976 and 1981.

Although small – the smallest garden in all of Paris – the square has an illustrious history. It once formed the entrance to a mansion owned by one of the most aristocratic families of the 17th and 18th centuries and, in the early 1800s, became an atelier for the neoclassical painter Jean-Auguste-Dominique Ingres (1780–1867), who had attended the École Nationale Supérieure des Beaux-Arts on nearby Rue Bonaparte.

Number 17 Rue Visconti was also where the novelist Honoré de Balzac (1799–1850) set up a printing press for two years, and a plaque honours his attempt. Dramatist Jean Racine lived at number 24, dying there in 1699, aged 59. And from 1835 to 1844, Eugène Delacroix (1798–1863) had a studio at number 19, where he painted Polish composer Frédéric Chopin (1810–1849) and his lover, the novelist George Sand (pen name of Amantine Lucile Aurore Dupin de Francueil, 1804–1876).

For all its artistic connections, this tiny space became a public square almost by accident. It was previously a council depot until the late 1990s, when a self-seeded tree took root. As it grew, the local inhabitants fought against its removal, forming the catalyst for the creation of a small green space for everyone to access.

The tree remains a central feature, and the square is paved with stone slabs around a central bed, which features Mexican orange blossom, ferns and periwinkles. There's also an oak pergola along the wall covered by ivy, honeysuckle and wisteria, and stone benches to sit on. The dappled shade creates a perfect spot in hotter months to sit and contemplate the area's considerable history.

54

7

HÔTEL DE L'ABBAYE

ADDRESS 10 Rue Cassette, 75006
HOURS Open to non-resident guests 2 p.m. to 9 p.m.
METRO Saint-Suplice

This hotel was originally a refuge for Bernardine nuns fleeing the Lorraine region of north-eastern France. They were offered protection in 1659 by Anne of Austria, mother of Louis XIV, and the abbey was originally known as the Monastery of Perpetual Adoration of the Blessed Sacrament. To this day, a drawing of a Benedictine sister resides in the hotel's entrance.

Its location, on a mostly residential street near the beautiful Jardin du Luxembourg, and close to the shops and restaurants of Saint-Germain-de-Prés – including the famous Les Deux Magots and Café de Flore (once frequented by Parisian intellectuals, writers, New Wave celebrities and fashion icons) – makes the hotel the perfect spot to stay. But it also boasts one of the most serene secret gardens of Paris, providing a retreat where you can indulge in an afternoon tea or an evening aperitif.

In the early 1990s, renowned French architect and designer Michel Boyer (1935–2011) worked with the original owners, Gisèle and Pierre-Antoine Lafortune, to redesign the hotel, with sumptuous decor, original paintings, ceramics and objets d'art, creating the atmosphere of the opulent 18th century and elevating it to a level of Parisian chic that ensures this 44-room hotel retains its four-star status.

The entrance on Rue Cassette is discreet, but just beyond the entrance and the hotel's lounge is a conservatory and walled courtyard, with seating comfortably arranged around small tables. The tranquillity of its ivied walls, small trees, shrubs and seasonal flower beds is enhanced by the background noise of running water from a walled fountain. The diffused daytime light and ambient evening lighting make this a secluded spot for the most romantic of rendezvous.

61

8

SQUARE ROGER-STÉPHANE

ADDRESS 7 Rue Juliette Récamier, 75007

HOURS 9.30 a.m. to 5.00 p.m., closed Tuesday

METRO Sèvres Babylone

Surrounded by residential buildings, and accessed by a pedestrian street running from the Rue de Sèvres, this secret garden is full of mature trees, including a majestic weeping beech at its centre, and was originally created in 1933.

One of the larger secret gardens, it measures 1,438 square metres and is landscaped on different levels, featuring raised beds full of mature shrubs and trees, including rhododendrons, lilacs and magnolia. There's a water feature near its entrance to welcome you into this extensive green sanctuary. And it's not far from the bustle of the Le Bon Marché department store and high-end shops such as Hermés – which is worth a visit itself, even if just to admire the tiled floor, the remnants of its previous life as a swimming pool.

The park was created in 1933 and originally named for the socialite Juliette Récamier (1777–1849), who was the muse of many artists and writers, among them Jacques-Louis David (1748–1825) and François-René de Chateaubriand (1768–1848). The original site was occupied by l'Abbaye-aux-Bois, a former Bernardine convent, where Récamier spent her last years. However, what remained of the convent was demolished in 1907 to extend the Rue de Sèvres, and in 2008, it was renamed in honour of the Resistance fighter, writer and gay rights activist Roger Stéphane (1919–1994).

At 6 Rue Juliette Récamier is an electrical substation, designed by the architect Paul Friesé (1851–1917), that was built in 1910 to supply the Métro. Disused since 1990, it became an EDF Foundation Space in 2008, designed to focus on nature, society and culture, and occasionally hosting temporary art exhibitions and other events. The EDF is the national electricity supplier.

The extensive foliage of the mature trees and shrubs gives this hidden park a particularly intimate feel, but at its far end is a small children's playground, reminding us how essential these green spaces are for local residents and their children, as well as for footsore visitors needing respite from the busy streets nearby.

73

9

MUSÉE BOURDELLE

ADDRESS 18 Rue Antoine Bourdelle, 75015

HOURS 10 a.m. to 6 p.m., closed Monday

METRO Montparnasse-Bienvenüe

Just north-west of Montparnasse cemetery is this extraordinary museum with two beautifully kept sculpture gardens – and admission is free. The museum is worth a visit in and of itself, but the gardens are really one of Paris's best-kept secrets.

Antoine Bourdelle (1861–1929) was a sculptor and teacher, and student of Auguste Rodin (1840–1917). He was also a teacher of both Alberto Giacometti (1901–1966) and Henri Matisse (1869–1954) at his renowned art academy. Bourdelle's studio is preserved, and the museum is home to many of his sculptures, graphic art and archive photographs, but it is the gardens that make this a considerable attraction.

The street-side garden is set along a cloistered wall, along which are numerous statues providing a backdrop to a huge bronze horse, a study for the monument to the Argentinian General Alvear. The gardens boast a multitude of plants and trees, including an Indian lilac and fig and apple trees, while clematis, roses, periwinkles, peonies, aquilegia and nepeta run the gamut of the seasons.

In the inner garden, a statue of Sappho with her harp sits beneath golden rain trees and *Paulownia* trees, and at her feet, a bed of ferns and geranium. While the *Dying Centaur* expires beneath a false acacia tree, another bronze, the *Virgin of the Offering*, holds the infant Christ aloft while looking down to the greenery below. Hellebore, honeysuckle, a climbing Iceberg rose, hydrangeas and Japanese anemones mean there is always something in flower in this lovely spot, with benches to relax and admire Bourdelle's extraordinary art.

Then there's the promenade. Almost a third garden, a green corridor along the back of the Plaster Casts Hall, flanked by a neat yew hedge and benches to sit and enjoy yet more sculptures. A Japanese maple, Mexican orange blossom and hydrangeas are all in evidence in this tranquil space.

Whether you are interested in horticulture or not, the care taken to ensure the beauty of these grounds throughout the year makes this one of the most pleasurable secret gardens to visit in Paris.

LEFT 'Sappho' by Antoine Bourdelle.

85

OPPOSITE BOTTOM LEFT 'Le Fruit' by Antoine Bourdelle.

OPPOSITE BOTTOM RIGHT 'Monument to General Alvear'
by Antoine Bourdelle.

92

LEFT 'Virgin of the Offering' by Antoine Bourdelle.

ABOVE LEFT 'Dying Centaur' by Antoine Bourdelle.

ABOVE RIGHT 'Muse en respect' fragment from the central motif of the frise from Théâtre des Champs-Elysées by Antoine Bourdelle (1910-13).

PREVIOUS 'Baigneuse Accroupie' by Antoine Bourdelle.

PREVIOUS View from café of inside garden of 'Dying Centaur'.

ABOVE 'Pointe de Grave' by Antoine Bourdelle.

RIGHT 'Muse en respect' fragment from the central motif of the frise from
Théâtre des Champs-Elysées by Antoine Bourdelle (1910-13).

ABOVE 'Premiere Victorie d'Hannibal' (1885).

RIGHT A 'Victoire' étude intermédiaire, allegorie du Monument au General Alvear (1913-23).

10

MUSÉE DU QUAI BRANLY –JACQUES CHIRAC

ADDRESS 37 Quai Jacques Chirac, 75007
Accessed also from 218 Rue de l'Université, 75007

HOURS 10.30 a.m. to 7 p.m, Tuesday to Sunday

METRO Iéna/Alma-Marceau

101

Jacques Chirac (1932–2019) was a former French politician, president (1995–2007) and prime minister (1974–76, 1986–88), and while this new museum had been proposed by many over the years, it was Chirac who brought the project to completion.

The museum's extensive collection of 307,000 works is curated to acknowledge the richness of culture and diversity that non-European civilisations have contributed to the world since Neolithic times. It opened in 2006 as the Musée du Quai Branly, after the street which had been named for the French scientist Édouard Branly (1844–1940), and was amended in 2016 to include Chirac's name.

The 1999 competition for the design was won by architect Jean Nouvel (b.1945), but equally important to its concept was the design of the 18,000 sq m garden by the influential botanist, designer and writer Gilles Clément (b.1943).

The initial concept of an 'invitation to travel' is inherent in its design and there are seven discrete gardens interlinked by paved pathways over different levels, with two water features. A vibrant, living wall of greenery on the side of the museum that faces the Quai Jacques Chirac seems to run the full length of the garden. A café at the garden's far end provides a spectacular view of the nearby Eiffel Tower, while also allowing visitors time to digest the full extent of this exceptional garden.

Around 30 plant species and 70 trees, including oaks and maples on the north side, and magnolias and cherry trees on the south, jostle alongside ornamental grasses, plantains, ferns, sedums, valerian, bamboos and a rose arbour to contribute to a varied floral landscape designed to reflect the museum's commitment to diversity and integration. Every year, in July and August, the garden hosts a festival, with cultural and other social events also utilising the open-air, semicircular amphitheatre at its heart.

Clément said, 'To make a garden, you need land and eternity.' As for the building's architect, Nouvel, he was very clear that the museum should emerge from the garden, that the edifice was integral to it – and served as more than a complement. In the creation of this space, they achieved one of the most accessible and abundant secret gardens in the city.

ABOVE RIGHT View of underside of Musée du Quai Branly - Jacques Chirac.

104

LEFT 'White futuristic' semi-dome used for outdoor festivals in the summer, as seen from the café terrace.

RIGHT BANK
RIVE DROITE

Historically, the Right Bank, or Rive Droite, was the wealthier side of the city, and originally home to many of Paris's high-end luxurious hotels clustered around the 1st and 8th arrondissements. Over time, it evolved. New and stylish boutique hotels, along with upmarket restaurants often offering international cuisine, began to open weekly in neighbourhoods ranging from Pigalle to Bastille.

A selection of the city's most iconic and cherished landmarks can also be found on the Rive Droite, including the Arc de Triomphe, the Champs-Élysées, the Louvre, the Sacré-Cœur Basilica in Montmartre, the Centre Pompidou (known colloquially as the Beaubourg), Les Halles, and the more bohemian Marais neighbourhood. Today, many believe the Right Bank reflects contemporary Paris better than the Left, as it is more ethnically and economically diverse.

Throughout the centuries, the Right Bank has served as the centre for banking and finance, including the stock market (Bourse) and various industrial activities. However, it also has a vibrant history of popular theatre and entertainment; Montmartre and Pigalle are known for their cabarets and lively performances that are more accessible than intellectual art.

The Rive Droite has its own distinct elegance, markedly different from the charm of the Rive Gauche. It is home to several renowned auction houses. The 8th arrondissement in particular boasts exclusive hotels, restaurants and art galleries, while luxury brands like Chanel, Gucci, Prada, Saint Laurent and Dior have their flagship stores on Avenue Montaigne. It is on this side of the river that you will also find the official residence of the French president, the 300-year-old Élysée Palace, which sits on Rue du Faubourg Saint-Honoré, rubbing shoulders with the flagship store of Lanvin, the offices of *Vogue France* and the Embassy of the United Kingdom.

11

PETIT PALAIS

ADDRESS Avenue Winston Churchill, 75008

HOURS 10 a.m. to 5.15 p.m., closed Mondays. Late opening Fridays.

METRO Champs–Elysées Clemenceau

The ornate and gilded Petit Palais was built in 1900 for the Exposition Universelle, or World's Fair, following a competition won by the architect Charles Girault (1851–1932), and it became the Musée des Beaux-Arts de la Ville de Paris in 1902. The permanent exhibition, which is free to access, includes many fine examples of art by Fragonard, Pissaro, Rembrandt, Monet, Vuillard and others. As befits such a majestic and important building, the surrounding gardens help showcase its splendour.

The inner courtyard boasts a particularly lovely secret garden, semicircular and beautifully verdant, with pampas grasses, cherry trees, *Acanthus*, *Euphorbia* and palms nestled inside a colonnaded walkway with a mosaic floor. Giandomenico Facchina (1826–1903) was the Italian mosaic artist responsible both for these floors and also for the surrounds of the three pools that shimmer in the centre of this idyllic spot.

Be sure to also look up at the beautiful frescos on the vaulted ceilings of the portico when you visit. These depict, and are entitled, 'The Months of the Year' and 'The Hours of the Day and Night', both by Paul Albert Baudoüin (1844–1931). He had studied under Pierre Puvis de Chavannes (1824–1898), who was well-known for his mural paintings.

The Petit Palais shares its beaux arts style with the equally ornate Pont Alexandre III (named in commemoration of the Franco-Russian alliance of 1892) nearby, also inaugurated for the Exposition Universelle. Its art nouveau lamps, four-winged and gilded horses on top of their plinths (representing the Arts, Sciences, Commerce and Industry), and copper nymphs all attest to the richness of Parisian art and culture.

It's perhaps for these reasons that the luxury fashion house Schiaparelli chooses the Petit Palais for its haute couture shows during Paris Fashion Week, creating another link to art, beauty and culture.

The garden provides an excellent escape from the pace of the nearby Champs-Élysées. Sit in one of the deckchairs to soak up the peaceful ambience, or enjoy a coffee or lunch from the Café le Jardin du Petit Palais.

124

12

PARC MONCEAU

ADDRESS 35 Boulevard de Courcelles, 75008

HOURS 7 a.m. to 10 p.m. in summer;
7 a.m. to 8 p.m. in winter

METRO Monceau

Parc Monceau is a 20-acre park situated in the prestigious 8th arrondissement, and has many secret aspects and artefacts to discover. It's also one of the few municipal parks where you're allowed on the grass.

The park was established at the instigation of a cousin of Louis XVI (1754–1793), Louis-Philippe d'Orléans, Duc de Chartres (1747–1793), both of whom were guillotined during the French Revolution (1789–1799). Louis-Philippe had bought the land and, in 1773, commissioned Louis Carrogis Carmontelle (1717–1806), a dramatist, painter and set designer, to create a garden, originally known as the Folie de Chartres. Along with trees, lawns, flower beds, statues, waterways and bridges, the park featured numerous 'follies', including a miniature Egyptian pyramid, a Roman colonnade, a Dutch windmill, a temple to Mars, an enchanted grotto and Italian vineyard, and other unexpected features for its aristocratic visitors to marvel at and enjoy.

By 1860, the park had been reduced in size and was purchased by the city, becoming one of the first public parks as part of the transformation of Paris by Georges-Eugène Haussmann (1809–1891), who was commissioned to carry out a huge project of urban renewal by Emperor Napoleon III (1808–1873).

The gated park has four wrought-iron gates tipped in gold, designed by Gabriel Davioud (1824–1881), who studied at the École des Beaux-Arts and worked closely with Haussmann on his mission to transform the city. In 1885, Davioud became chief architect for the city's parks and public spaces.

The park's beauty has also been captured in the paintings of Claude Monet (1840–1926), who created a series of three paintings in 1876, and Gustave Caillebotte (1848–1894). It was a favourite haunt of Marcel Proust (1871–1922), who lived at 45 Rue de Courcelles and often played there as a child.

Today, it's popular with local residents and visitors alike, all keen to take advantage of its extensive green space, picnic opportunities, children's playground, café and free WiFi. You could visit this beautiful park a dozen times and still find new secret places to explore and enjoy.

139

13

MUSÉE DE LA VIE ROMANTIQUE

ADDRESS 16 Rue Chaptal, 75009

HOURS 10 a.m. to 6 p.m., closed Mondays
(Closed for renovations until early spring 2026)

METRO Pigalle/Blanche

141

The Museum of Romantic Life was once the private home and atelier of Ary Scheffer (1795–1858), a painter of the Romantic school who often used the work of Byron, Goethe, Walter Scott and Dante as his subject. He and his illustrious contemporaries were intellectuals and artists, including the painter Eugène Delacroix and composer Frédéric Chopin, who often met at this garden.

The house remained a private home until the late 1980s and opened as the museum we see today following the 1987 renovations of Jacques Garcia (b.1947), a designer renowned for the interiors of many upmarket and opulent hotels, and very sensitive to the Romantic style and ambience.

The museum's permanent collection contains many artworks, sculptures, artefacts and memorabilia that reflect the Romantic period. It is also an archive of items associated with the novelist George Sand. Greatly admired by Victor Hugo, Gustave Flaubert and Sand, she wrote 70 novels, plus plays and extensive essays, and was a great champion of women's rights. As the museum is owned by the city of Paris, it is free to access.

The charming and secluded garden is accessed by a paved and tree-lined alley leading off Rue Chaptal. Abundant roses in the summer months, hydrangeas, hollyhocks, alliums, mock orange and lilac, ivy and clematis on the walls, a circular bed, statues and multiple potted shrubs and plants make this the epitome of the Romantic movement's fascination with the beauty of nature.

As well as its historical significance, the Museum of Romantic Life offers an incredibly immersive and olfactory experience. This is enhanced visually by the early morning and late afternoon sunlight. The laughter and shrieks of school children playing, accompanied by birdsong, makes time spent in this garden uniquely memorable.

Originally the painting studio of Cornelia Scheffer, the external glasshouse is now a tea room, the Rose Bakery, where you can enjoy a morning coffee, light lunch or afternoon tea. It's easy to imagine the salons of days gone by when Scheffer, his artist daughter Cornelia, and their friends met to discuss the current artistic, cultural and political events of their time.

150

14

LE JARDIN VIVIENNE, BNF RICHELIEU

ADDRESS 5 Rue Vivienne, 75002

HOURS Varies each day

METRO Bourse

155

Located in the second arrondissement behind the Palais Royal and French Comedy Theatre, is part of the recently renovated National Library BNF Richelieu. The entrance is directly opposite one of Paris's most well-known passages, Gallery Vivienne, which is an 18th century undercover arcade with boutiques, restaurants and galleries.

Le Jardin Vivienne was recently completely renovated and redesigned by the influential botanist, designer and writer Gilles Clément (b.1943), who was responsible for the garden at Musée du Quai Branly – Jacques Chirac. Its concept, in collaboration with heritage architect Mirabelle Croizier and landscape designer Antoine Quenardel, was to symbolically tell the story of the future while drawing on its history.

Reflecting the nature of the BNF's commitment to the storage and preservation of all forms of paperwork from manuscripts to books, this standout garden harbours the secrets of a *hortus papyrifer*, or paper garden. Plants were meticulously selected to represent the connection between the garden and the bibliothèque, and include the paper mulberry, papyrus, bamboo, rice-paper plant, palms and banana plants, along with small trees like the birch and cherry, which have a paper-like bark. This is all intentionally designed to co-exist closely in a visual juxtaposition, a style which significantly influenced the Renaissance art movement.

The garden is an increasingly lush and glorious green courtyard, with numerous beds and secluded areas, its secrets well worth exploring. There are several restored marble Medici vases nestled in the side of the garden, as well as two marble fire pots – one being the centrepiece of the main garden path. The BNF's on-site café makes this a perfect place to meet friends, sit reading or meditate on the garden's relevance and beauty.

Le Jardin Vivienne is worth visiting any month, and you should factor in time to explore the library, which is open to the public. For me, it's particularly magical in September, when the metre-high grasses are in full bloom. This sea of fluffy white plants that glow with the sun's soft light is truly a hypnotic spectacle to behold.

160

15

MUSÉE CARNAVALET

ADDRESS 23 Rue de Sévigné, 75003

HOURS 10 a.m. to 6 p.m., closed Mondays

METRO Saint Paul

167

Located in the Marais, not far from the Picasso Museum, this former private home is dedicated to the history of Paris, from prehistoric times to the present day. It's an extraordinarily rich and diverse collection, and among its 618,000 items, such as paintings, furniture, sculptures, shop signs, historical artefacts and photographs, are recreated period rooms and personal items that once belonged to historical figures like Napoleon I (1769–1821) and Marcel Proust.

The museum began life as a private mansion for Jacques des Ligneris (1480–1556), president of the Parliament of Paris. It underwent various reincarnations, but became the property of the city in 1866 and was formally named a museum of the history of Paris in 1880. Various expansions and restorations, both of the building and of many of its exhibits, continued. Its most recent was completed in 2022 following a five-year closure and upgrade at the cost of €55 million.

This revamping also included renovation of the internal courtyards and two beautifully landscaped gardens, in keeping with the style of the museum. Formal beds with boxwoods pruned into swirling shapes showcase roses and other flowering plants, shrubs and greenery. It's a serene space, enhanced by the elegant tables and chairs of the Fabula restaurant, which is open between May and October and available for private dining. Here, you can sit in the soft light of the limestone architecture, overlooked by the statue of Victory, a winged angel holding two olive wreaths aloft in her hands, the work of Louis-Simon Boizot (1743–1809), while enjoying a summer cocktail.

In acknowledgement to these icons of Parisian heritage, there is also a recently installed Wallace drinking fountain (see the entry on Square Laurent-Prache for more information), dispensing clean water from which to refill a bottle or glass. Originally sited on Place Denfert-Rochereau, a public square in the 14th arrondissement, this fountain features four caryatids symbolising goodness, sobriety, simplicity and charity.

Like many hidden Parisian gardens, this one benefits from the beautiful architecture of a once-private home, and is now a public space for everyone to enjoy.

ABOVE Wallace Fountain (1 of 107 in Paris) by Charles-Auguste Lebourg, made in the late 1800s.

ABOVE LEFT Detail of the main gate entrance of the museum.

ABOVE RIGHT Louis Simon Boizot's 'Victoire' sculpture.

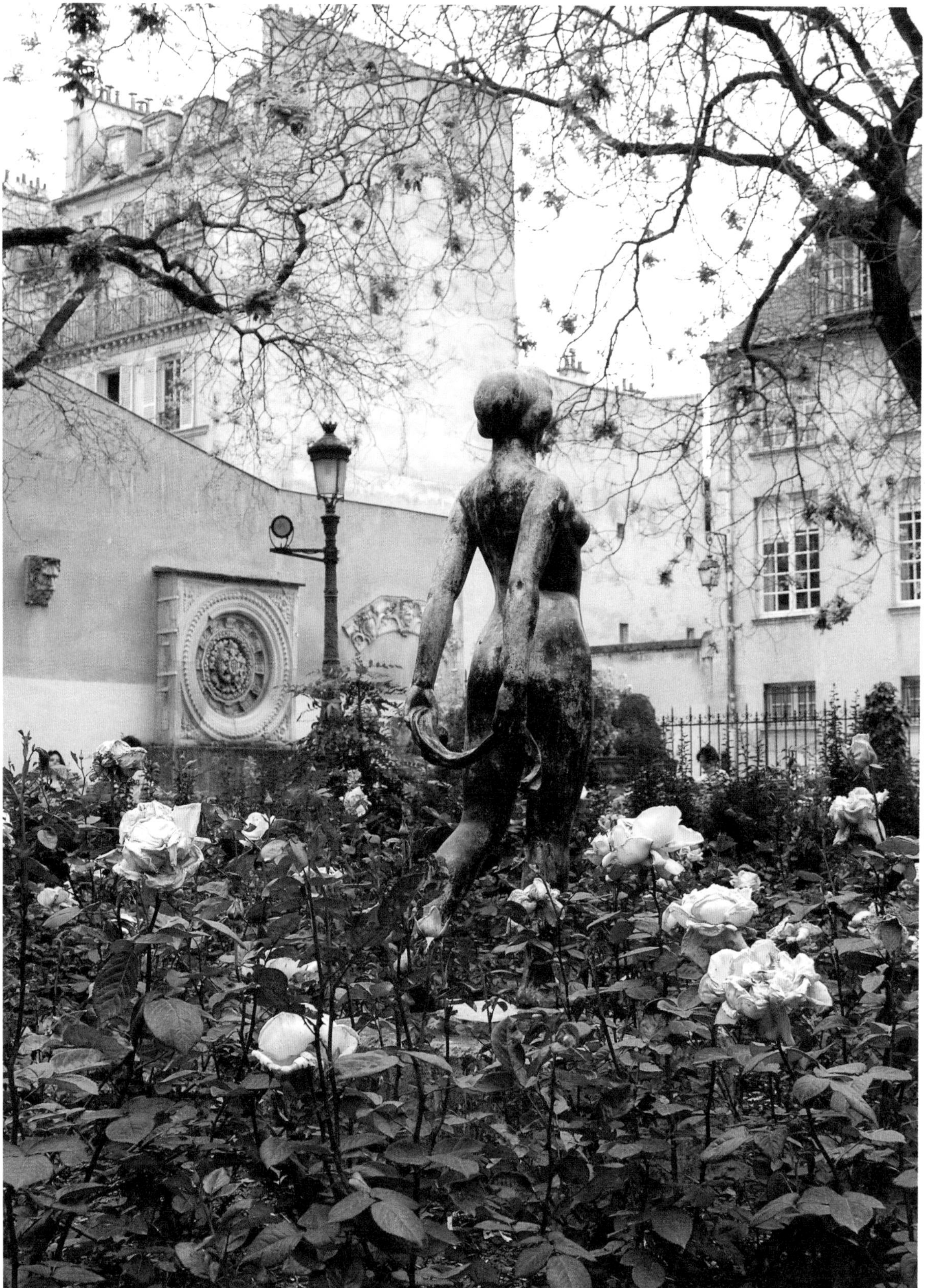

16

SQUARE GEORGES CAIN

ADDRESS 8 Rue Payenne, 75003
HOURS 9 a.m. to 5.00 p.m, closed Tuesdays
METRO Saint Paul/Chemin Vert

Square Georges Cain is a small, hidden garden that feels like an open-air museum. Located in a quiet street in the Marais, it is so-named to commemorate Georges Cain (1856–1919), a painter, illustrator and writer, and curator at the Musée Carnavalet between 1897 and 1914.

With a row of small pollarded trees along one side, the square prides itself on its century-old fig tree: it has a gnarled trunk, but shows every sign of being in good health. Silver birch trees, bay trees in planters and sculpted cypresses provide further foliage, and the flower beds are abundant in summer where roses, acanthus, foxgloves and other seasonal plants all grace the square.

From a circular rose bed at its centre rises one of six bronze casts by sculptor Aristide Maillol (1861–1944). The sculpture depicts a nude female bather, representing the Île-de-France (an original marble is in the Musée d'Orsay), the region of France that claims Paris as its capital. And when the wind blows, you may be surprised to hear a nightingale sing, the electronic work of sound artist Erik Samakh (b.1959). In contrast to this view, at the far left of the garden, stands the aforementioned

100-year-old fig tree. With its sprawling trunk, rising above a lush wild bed of vegetation, this incredible tree adds to the square's rich offerings.

There are also unexpected treasures to be found, and an array of architectural remnants feature on the far wall of the square. At the centre of the wall, there is a portico from the long-destroyed Tuileries Palace, including its columns and a clock face. Other relics include a salt storehouse, a Renaissance-era rose window from the old Hôtel de Ville, a window from the Hôtel de Thou, and even fragments of Merovingian sarcophagi. This is truly a unique experience in Paris, as this style of open-air space is much more typical of Athens.

Quieter during the week, this discreet square is a real find: somewhere to take a pause in your day, but also a chance to admire Paris's long history of architectural conservation and garden creation. This is also a popular local park for canine owners, and is particularly lively at the weekend. Here, you will find a mix of Parisians and expats living in the quieter part of Le Parais, taking a break in a green space complete with ancient Parisian relics.

175

LEFT Original Renaissance rose window from the old Hôtel de Ville of Paris.

ABOVE Original relic from the Tuilleries Palace, the 'Tympan orné de deux Victoires'.

ABOVE The 100-year-old fig tree in the far right of the garden, visible from the street.

RIGHT Various original relics from 18th-century Paris create an outdoor museum.

184

17

JARDIN LAZARE RACHLINE

ADDRESS 9 Rue Payenne, 75003
HOURS 10 a.m. to 5 p.m., closed Tuesdays
METRO Saint Paul

As one of the smaller secret gardens in Paris, with just six benches – and no dogs allowed – Jardin Lazare Rachline is often peacefully quiet, a welcome break from the hustle and bustle of the surrounding streets of the Marais district.

The garden is named after Lazare Rachline (1905–1968), an industrialist and businessman of Russian origin who was committed to antisemitism and served as a member of the Resistance during the Vichy regime of the Second World War. However, the garden square is a more recent feature, having been created in 1974, after its purchase by the city of Paris. Located in the courtyard of the Hôtel Donon, which became home to the Musée Cognacq-Jay in 1990, this museum showcases a fine collection of 18th-century art.

Although relatively modern, this well-tended garden is designed in a formal way, with yew hedges lining the three walls that surround it, while the main grassy area and flower beds are edged with trimmed boxwood, embellished by cone-shaped cypresses. Mature rose bushes and seasonal planting mean a pretty display of flowers, floral shrubs and other plants, around which the gravel paths meander.

It's the sort of garden you might stumble on unawares, en route from A to B, but once you do, you will want to return – which is probably why the local residents would prefer to keep it a secret.

185

186

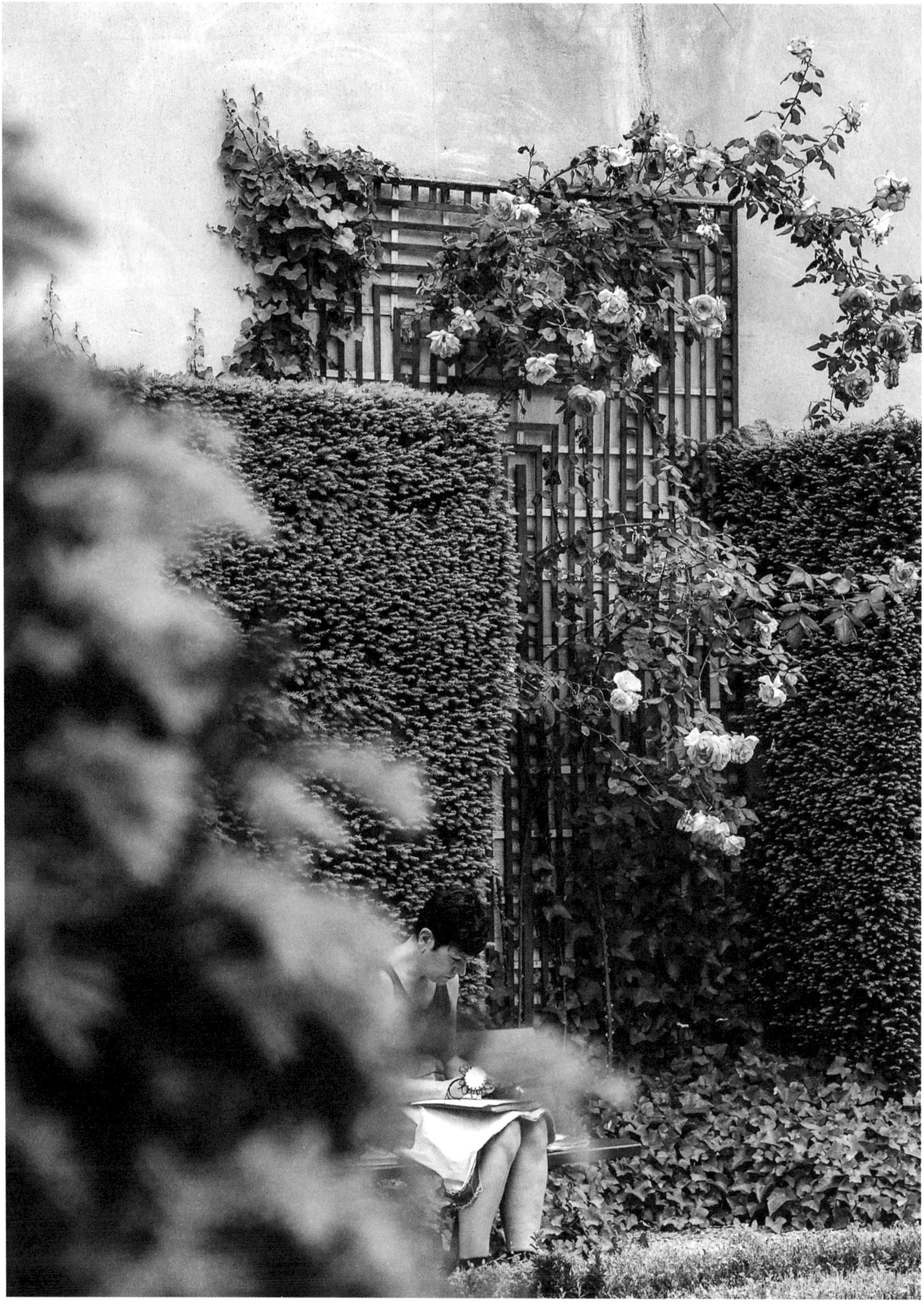

18

LE PAVILLON DE LA REINE

ADDRESS 28 Place des Vosges, 75003

HOURS Open to non-residents at the discretion of the management

METRO Chemin Vert

The *reine* in question is Anne of Austria (1601–1666), a former queen of France and the mother of Louis XIV (1638–1715), who lived in a wing of the building. Le Pavillon was built as a royal palace in 1612 and, given its central and prestigious location, soon became something of a resort for high-society gatherings, attracting the celebrated writers Jean-Baptiste Racine (1639–1699), Molière (1622–1673) and Jean de La Fontaine (1621–1695).

It's through the domed arcades of Place de Vosges that you'll find the courtyard entrance to the hotel, inviting and especially prettily lit at dusk. The paved garden is through the hotel, set well back from the street, lending it a calm and intimate ambience even on the busiest days.

Here, non-residents can find peace from the pedestrians and traffic of the Marais and enjoy the intimate shade of small Japanese maples, elegant boxwood hedges and pretty topiary, white hydrangeas and lilacs, ivied walls and sweetly scented jasmine, graced by a contemporary statue of a sylphlike young dancer. The Michelin-starred restaurant Anne ensures this is a perfect place for morning coffee, a discreet rendezvous or an evening cocktail before dinner.

The Place des Vosges has its own beauty: its gated square with formal trees surrounded by the arcades of the buildings which house numerous boutiques, art galleries and restaurants. At the centre of the square is an equestrian statue of Louis XIII (1601–1643) depicted as a Roman emperor with a laurel wreath atop his head. Four large and identical fountains, one at each corner of the square, were made by the same sculptor, Jean-Pierre Cortot (1787–1843), and installed in 1825.

Those who are *au courant* with the quiet luxury of this delightful garden tend to keep it to themselves, but once you know, you know.

191

OVERLEAF RIGHT 'La Marathonienne' by Philippe Hiquily (1981).

19

COULÉE VERTE RENÉ-DUMONT

ADDRESS Avenue Daumesnil to Avenue Émile-Laurent, 75012

HOURS 8/9 a.m. to 5.45 p.m. in autumn and winter, 8 a.m. to 9.30 p.m. in spring and summer

METRO Porte Dorée

An extraordinary 4.5-km route that utilises a disused 1859 railway line linking the Place de la Bastille to the Bois des Vincennes, the Coulée Verte René-Dumont was originally called the Promenade Plantée, and was created by architect Philippe Mathieux (b. 1945) and landscape architect Jacques Vergely. Construction started in 1988 and it was inaugurated in 1993. Named after René Dumont (1904–2001), a pioneering agronomist, economist and environmentalist, the Coulée Verte blends nature with the city's historic and more recent architecture, and was the inspiration for New York City's High Line.

This green walkway, elevated for much of its length, runs from an entry point where the Rue de Lyon meets the Avenue Daumesnil behind the Opéra Bastille, and east to Avenue Émile-Laurent, where the descent is via a spiral staircase close to the Boulevard Périphérique, with numerous access points along its route.

Following the old railway route, the Coulée Verte combines wild vegetation with more formal landscaping, featuring copious lime and hazelnut trees, climbing roses and other flowering plants. Starting at the famous

and revamped Viaduc des Arts – all glass-fronted galleries, workshops and boutiques under its arches – then crossing Boulevard Diderot and running over the Jardin de Reuilly on a suspension bridge to the tree-lined Allée Vivaldi, the journey provides a captivating impression of this area of the city. At its highest, the Coulée Verte is 10 metres off the ground; sometimes it cuts through buildings and at others opens to extensive views.

Favoured by local runners and walkers – dogs are allowed if kept on a leash – this green belt offers a particularly diverse view of the 12th arrondissement, and is perfect for those who want to experience the well-executed blending of an urban environment with a rural oasis.

LEFT City council building with series of replica statues of
Michaelangelo's 'Dying Slave', visible from the Coulée Verte.

RIGHT Public art along the Coulée Verte René-Dumont.

LEFT View of the unique aspect of the Coulée Verte stairs, where the path cuts through a building.

210

20

JARDIN DES ROSIERS JOSEPH MIGNERET

ADDRESS 10 Rue des Rosiers, 75004

HOURS 8/9 a.m. to 5.15 p.m. in the autumn and winter, 8 a.m. to 6 p.m. in the spring and summer

METRO Saint-Paul

211

Hidden away from the shops, restaurants and hotels of the busy Marais, it would be easy to miss the entrance to this garden on Rue des Rosiers, via a narrow lane lined with remnants of the old city wall of Paris, known as the Wall of Philippe Auguste (1165–1223), king of France from 1180 until his death.

The principal of a local school, Joseph Migneret (1888–1949) was instrumental in saving many local Jewish children from deportation, hiding them or securing forged papers, and it is he who is honoured in the name of this peaceful garden.

Originally the private gardens of three 17th-century mansions – Hôtel de Coulanges, Maison Barbès and Hôtel d'Albret – this enclosed space is 1,095 square metres. Although surrounded by residential buildings, the garden is open and light-filled, and has been transformed into three distinct areas, created by landscape gardener Marie-Odile Ricard and rated as one of Paris's EcoJardin. Both a public space and a community garden, the Jardin des Rosiers Joseph Migneret has well-organised volunteers who can be found working there on a Saturday morning.

There is an orchard and a vegetable garden, with a remarkable fig tree and a chestnut tree, flanked by *Ceanothus* plants in one area. Another section is populated by grasses and ferns reminiscent of swamp landscapes – a nod to the fact that the historical meaning of the word 'Marais' is 'swamp'. Vines crawl up one wall and old espaliered trees another, transforming this urban area into a green space much loved by its locals.

Children have a space here that caters to them, with a wooden boat to play on and several animal figures on the grass among the silver birch trees. This gesture to youth is highlighted in a large memorial plaque displaying the names of 100 infants and children, the youngest just 27 days old, who were deported to Auschwitz between 1942 and 1944.

There is much to discover of Paris's commitment to its communities through its green spaces. And this one, like all the gardens, squares and paths explored in this book, provides an opportunity to meander, meditate on life's mysteries or chat with a friend, all while surrounded by the living, breathing fusion of history and nature in a modern city.

217

ACKNOWLEDGEMENTS

The idea behind the book emerged in its current form around 2020 and germinated in the background of my creative projects for a few more years. As a freelance photographer, I believe that timing is everything, and so the project gained momentum in 2023.

First and foremost, I would like to express my gratitude to Kirstie Armiger-Grant at Hardie Grant Australia for her invaluable guidance and feedback on preparing my book proposal, as well as for referring me to Kate Pollard and the UK office. An immense and heartfelt thank you to Kate, my publisher, for not only sharing my enthusiasm for this idea from the very beginning but also for believing in my work and recognizing its full potential to making it happen! Most importantly, thank you for granting me the creative freedom at every step of the process.

I would also like to thank Phoebe Bath, Kate's amazing assistant editor, who has seamlessly managed the delivery of my content and provided invaluable support throughout my many emails. Thank you also to Evi-O.Studio and Eloise Myatt, for the wonderful design of the book itself.

A special mention to my dear friend Mara, who introduced me to the magical and secret garden of Pavilion de la Reine, where we often retreat on a hot summer afternoon for our heartfelt and creative catchups.

Thank you to Hotel L'Abbaye and Pavilion de la Reine for accepting my proposal and entrusting me with capturing the essence of their beautiful gardens.

Lastly, thank you, Paris, for choosing me to live here and encouraging me to discover your unique essence via the secret gardens.

221

ABOUT THE AUTHOR

Elli Ioannou is an international, award-winning fashion photographer, photomedia artist, mentor and educator based Wto Paris in 2016 for personal and professional growth. That same year, she became the Paris correspondent for Paris Fashion Week with D.A.M magazine.

With over 17 years' experience as a fashion photographer, Elli has also written and delivered fashion photography and film programs in undergraduate and masters' level degrees in Australia and in Paris, including Paris College of Art and Parsons Paris.

Elli's fashion photography has appeared in premium public and trade magazines in both Europe and Australia. Notable international distinctions for her photomedia artwork include the Luciano Benetton Imago Mundi permanent collection and book: *Looking Down Under: Contemporary Artists from Australia* (2015). Elli has also held several solo and group exhibitions in Australia and Europe.

Working at Paris Fashion Week was Elli's gateway to discovering Paris from a unique perspective: from historical and modern architecture, to learning about fashion as art, and design, all had the same quality in Elli's eye – beauty. This is the aesthetic that has been the subject of many of Elli's exhibitions and is at the heart of her creative practice.

Quadrille, Penguin Random House UK,
One Embassy Gardens, 8 Viaduct Gardens,
London SW11 7BW

Quadrille Publishing Limited is part of the Penguin Random
House group of companies whose addresses can be found at
global.penguinrandomhouse.com

Published by Quadrille in 2025
www.penguin.co.uk

A CIP catalogue record for this book is available
from the British Library

ISBN 978-1-78488-977-7

10 9 8 7 6 5 4 3 2 1

Publishing Director – Kate Pollard
Editor – Harriet Griffey
Assistant Editor – Phoebe Bath
Designer – Evi-O.Studio | Eloise Myatt
Production Controller – Martina Georgieva

Colour reproduction by p2d
Printed in China by RR Donnelley Asia Printing Solution Limited

The authorised representative in the EEA is Penguin
Random House Ireland, Morrison Chambers,
32 Nassau Street, Dublin D02 YH68.